# CYRANO
# de Bergerac

## Edmond Rostand

Abridged and adapted by Tony Napoli

Illustrated by Gershom Griffith

A PACEMAKER CLASSIC

GLOBE FEARON

Pearson Learning Group

**Executive Editor:** Joan Carrafiello
**Project Editor:** Karen Bernhaut
**Editorial Assistant:** Keisha Carter
**Production Director:** Penny Gibson
**Print Buyer:** Cheryl Johnson
**Production Editor:** Alan Dalgleish
**Desktop Specialist:** Margarita T. Linnartz
**Art Direction:** Joan Jacobus
**Marketing Manager:** Marge Curson
**Cover and Interior Illustrations:** Gershom Griffith
**Cover Design:** Margarita T. Linnartz

ISBN 0-8359-1399-6
Printed in the United States of America

14 15 16 V036 15 14

Globe
Fearon

Pearson Learning Group

1-800-321-3106
www.pearsonlearning.com

# Contents

# Cast of Characters

CYRANO DE BERGERAC — A soldier, poet, philosopher, and scientist. He has an enormous nose and is very sensitive about it.

CHRISTIAN DE NEUVILLETTE — Cyrano's comrade-in-arms

ROXANE (MADELEINE ROBIN) — A beautiful young woman with whom both Cyrano and Christian are in love

COUNT DE GUICHE — The nephew of the powerful Cardinal Richelieu. Although already married, he loves Roxane, too.

LE BRET — Cyrano's friend and adviser

RAGUENEAU — A poet who runs a bakery shop where other poets meet

LISE — Ragueneau's wife

LIGNIÈRE — A poet and Cyrano's friend

VALVERT — A man who insults Cyrano by referring to his nose

MONTFLEURY — An actor who has angered Cyrano

CARBON DE CASTEL-JALOUX — The captain of the Gascony Guards

MOTHER MARGUÉRITE DE JÉSUS — Mother Superior at the convent where Roxane goes to live

SISTER MARTHE AND SISTER CLAIRE — Nuns at the same convent

# ACT 1

## A Performance at the Hôtel de Bourgogne

*The play takes place in Paris, France, in the year 1640. Act 1 opens in a theater in the Hôtel de Bourgogne. The audience is waiting for that evening's play to begin. Among the audience are a poet, a baker, several marquises (noblemen), and a young newcomer to the city named Christian.*

*The lead actor in that night's play is Montfluery. When he takes the stage, he is interrupted by the voice of a man offstage. The man is Cyrano de Bergerac. He has a personal grudge against Montfluery and demanded that he not take the stage for a month. Cyrano forces Montfluery off the stage.*

*Then Cyrano fights a duel with an arrogant nobleman who insults him. The crowd, once against Cyrano, rallies to his side when he defeats the nobleman with wit and grace.*

## Scene 1

*The theater in the Hôtel de Bourgogne. The audience begins to arrive. Gentlemen, a tradesman, pages, thieves, and the* DOORKEEPER *enter, followed by* THE ORANGE GIRL *and violinists. Loud voices are heard from outside. Two* GENTLEMEN *enter suddenly.*

DOORKEEPER: Stop! You haven't paid your money.

FIRST GENTLEMAN: I come in free!

DOORKEEPER: Why?

FIRST GENTLEMAN: I belong to the king's cavalry.

DOORKEEPER (*to the* SECOND GENTLEMAN)*:* And you?

SECOND GENTLEMAN: I don't pay either!

DOORKEEPER: Why?

SECOND GENTLEMAN: I'm a musketeer!

FIRST GENTLEMAN: The play does not begin until two o'clock. The house is empty. Let's try our foils. (*They fence with the foils they've brought.*)

TRADESMAN (*leading his son in*): Let's sit here.

GAMBLER: Aces!

TRADESMAN (*to his son*): You would think this was some evil place, wouldn't you? (*The fencers separate, and one of them knocks him over.*) Fighters over here! (*He falls among the card players.*) Gamblers over there! To think that famous plays have been performed in such places as this, my son.

YOUNG MAN (*to his father*): What's the name of the play?

TRADESMAN: *Clorise.*

YOUNG MAN: Whose work is it?

TRADESMAN: Mr. Baro's. 'Tis a piece! (*Walks off, taking his son's arm*) You'll see the most famous actors—Montfleury, Bellerose, and Jodelet!

PAGE (*in the hall*): Ah, here's the Orange Girl!

THE ORANGE GIRL: Oranges, milk, raspberry syrup, lemonade!

(*The Marquis* CUIGY *and* BRISSAILLE *enter.*)

BRISSAILLE (*seeing that the hall is half empty*): How's this? Do we arrive early like tradesmen, without disturbing people, without stepping on their feet?

CUIGY: Yes, we've come before the candles have been lighted.

BRISSAILLE: I'm so annoyed. . .

CUIGY: Cheer up. Here comes the lighter.

(*The lighter of the chandeliers enters.* THE CROWD *gathers around the chandeliers as they are lighted.*)

# Scene 2

*The theater in the Hôtel de Bourgogne.* LIGNIÈRE *and* CHRISTIAN DE NEUVILLETTE *enter, arm in arm.* CHRISTIAN'S *attention is elsewhere, and he looks at the boxes.* RAGENEAU *and* LE BRET *enter.*

CUIGY: Lignière!

LIGNIÈRE (*aside, to* CHRISTIAN): Shall I introduce you? (CHRISTIAN *nods.*) Christian de Neuvillette, please meet Mr. Cuigy and Mr. Brissaille.

CHRISTIAN (*bowing*): Delighted to meet you, gentlemen.

CUIGY (*to* BRISSAILLE, *looking at* CHRISTIAN): He has a charming face!

LIGNIÈRE (*to* CUIGY): He's just arrived from Touraine.

CHRISTIAN: Yes, I've been in Paris only three weeks. I'm joining the guards tomorrow, as a cadet.

CUIGY (*to* CHRISTIAN, *pointing to the hall as it begins to fill*): A crowd!

CHRISTIAN: Yes, quite.

LIGNIÈRE (*taking* CHRISTIAN *aside*): My friend, I came here to help you. But since the lady has not arrived, I shall go.

CHRISTIAN (*pleading*): No, stay! You, who sings of the city and court. You will tell me for whom I am dying of love.

THE ORANGE GIRL: Cookies, lemonade. . .

(*The violins begin to play.*)

CHRISTIAN: I'm afraid the lady is rather proper. I dare not talk to her. I'm only a shy soldier. I have no wit.

LIGNIÈRE (*preparing to leave*): I really must go.

CHRISTIAN (*holding him back*): No, stay!

LIGNIÈRE: Because you insist, I'll wait a little longer.

THE CROWD (*greeting a fat and beaming little man as he enters*): Ah, Ragueneau!

LIGNIÈRE (*to* CHRISTIAN): There's Ragueneau, the great baker.

RAGUENEAU (*dressed like a pastry cook, hurrying toward* LIGNIÈRE): Sir, have you seen Cyrano?

LIGNIÈRE (*introducing* RAGUENEAU *to* CHRISTIAN): This is Ragueneau, the pastry cook of actors and poets!

RAGUENEAU (*embarrassed*): You honor me too much. (*Looks all around*) Cyrano isn't here? I'm surprised.

**4**

LIGNIÈRE: Why?

RAGUENEAU: Montfleury is in the play!

LIGNIÈRE: But what does it matter to Cyrano?

RAGUENEAU: Haven't you heard? He took a dislike to Montfleury. He ordered him not to appear on the stage for a month.

CHRISTIAN: Who is this Cyrano?

CUIGY: A lad well-skilled with a sword. He's a cadet in the Guards. But his friend Le Bret can tell you. . .(*Shouts*) Le Bret! (LE BRET *comes over.*) You're looking for Cyrano de Bergerac, too?

LE BRET: Yes, and I'm concerned. . .

CUIGY: He's an uncommon man, isn't he?

LE BRET: The most delightful of men.

RAGUENEAU: A poet!

CUIGY: A swordsman!

BRISSAILLE: A scientist!

LE BRET: A musician!

LIGNIÈRE: And what a strange appearance!

RAGUENEAU: With his triple-plumed hat, his cape flowing behind his rising sword. . . and his nose. Ah, what a nose! Those who see it can't help saying, "No, it can't be true. He'll soon take it off."

LE BRET: He keeps it on—and runs his sword through anyone who looks at it too closely.

(*Words of admiration from the crowd.* ROXANE

*has just appeared in her box. She sits in the front; her chaperon sits in the rear.*)

CHRISTIAN (*looks up, sees* ROXANE, *and grabs* LIGNIÈRE's *arm*): There she is!

LIGNIÈRE (*looking*): Ah, is she the one?

CHRISTIAN: Yes, tell me quickly who she is.

LIGNIÈRE: Madeleine Robin, known as Roxane. She's smart, witty, and free, an orphan and a cousin of Cyrano, whom we were just discussing.

(*At this moment, a well-dressed nobleman enters* ROXANE's *box and stands talking with her for a few moments.*)

CHRISTIAN: Who is that man?

LIGNIÈRE: That is the Count de Guiche. He is in love with her. But he's married to Cardinal Richelieu's niece. He wants Roxane to marry the Viscount de Valvert, a sorry example of a man. Valvert will agree and allow de Guiche to see her whenever he wishes. She is against it, but de Guiche is powerful.

CHRISTIAN: I'm leaving. I'm going to pay a visit to the Viscount de Valvert!

LIGNIÈRE: No, *I'm* leaving. I'm thirsty—and I'm expected in the taverns. (*He leaves.*)

THE CROWD: Let the play begin!

(DE GUICHE *comes down from* ROXANE's *box. He is surrounded by noblemen, one of whom is* VALVERT.)

DE GUICHE: I am going on the stage. Come, Valvert!

(CHRISTIAN *starts when he hears* VALVERT's *name.*)

CHRISTIAN: Valvert! I will throw in his face my— (*He puts his hand in his pocket and feels the hand of a* THIEF.) What's this?

THIEF: Oh, no! Let me go, and I'll tell you a secret.

CHRISTIAN: What is it?

THIEF: Lignière, who just left you. . . is about to meet his death. A song he wrote offended some great person. A hundred men—I am one—will lie in wait tonight.

CHRISTIAN: Where will you all be waiting for him?

THIEF: At the Porte de Nesle. On his way home, we'll attack. Warn him!

CHRISTIAN: Yes, I will go! Oh, you rascals. A hundred men against one! (*He runs out.*)

THE CROWD: Begin the play!

(*A bagpipe song is heard. The very fat* MONTFLEURY *appears on the stage. He is wearing a shepherd's costume and is blowing into a bagpipe.*)

THE CROWD (*applauding*): Montfleury! Bravo!

MONTFLEURY (*bowing*): "Happy is he who shuns the pomp of courts. . ."

A VOICE (*from the middle of the floor*): Rascal, didn't I forbid it for a month?

(*There's surprise in the audience. Those in the boxes stand up to see.*)

LE BRET (*terrified*): It is Cyrano!

THE VOICE OF CYRANO: Off the stage at once, king of buffoons.

MONTFLUERY: But. . .

THE VOICE OF CYRANO: You refuse?

VARIOUS VOICES IN THE CROWD: Go on, Montfleury! Don't be afraid!

MONTFLUERY (*in a hesitating voice*): "Happy is he who shuns. . ."

THE VOICE OF CYRANO: Off the stage!

MONFLUERY (*choking*): "Happy is he. . ."

CYRANO (*standing up on a chair with his arms folded. His hat is cocked to one side, and his nose stands out strongly.*): I shall be angry.

# Scene 3

*The theater in the Hôtel de Bourgogne.* CYRANO *approaches the stage.*

CYRANO (*to* MONTFLUERY): Leave the stage. (THE CROWD *closes in with an angry sound.*) Does anyone object? (*They draw back again.*)

THE CROWD: The play! The play!

CYRANO: I command you to be silent. And I challenge you all. Come. I will write down your names! Draw near, young heroes! Who wants to be at the top of the list? (*Silence*) Not one finger? Very good. I will go on. (*He turns back toward the stage where* MONTFLUERY *has been waiting in agony.*) I wish to see the theater cured of swelling. If not—the scalpel! (*He draws his sword.*)

9

MONTFLEURY: I—

CYRANO (*sits down in the middle of the circle that has formed around him*): I'm going to clap my hands three times. By the third clap, you will be gone. One! (*Claps*)

MONTFLEURY: Gentlemen, I believe. . .

CYRANO: Two! (*Claps again*)

MONTFLEURY: I'm sure it would be better—

CYRANO: Three! (*Claps a third time*)

(MONTFLEURY *disappears. Howls of laughter, hisses, and boos*)

THE CROWD: Boo! Coward, come back!

(BELLEROSE *and* JODELET, *two other actors, come forward and bow.*)

THE CROWD: Ah! Here are Bellerose and Jodelet!

BELLEROSE: What about the money that must be given back?

CYRANO (*turns toward the stage*): Now, that's the first wise thing that's been said. Far be it for me to bring hardship on those practicing the art of acting. (*Stands up and throws a bag on the stage*) Here, take this purse and be quiet.

JODELET (*quickly picking up the purse and weighing it in his hand*): At this price, sir, I'll be glad to have you come everyday and stop our performances!

THE CROWD: Boo! Boo!

JODELET: Even if we are all booed together!

BELLEROSE: Please clear the hall.

JODELET: Everyone out, please.

(*The audience begins to leave. But the crowd soon comes back in. The women in the boxes sit down again.*)

LE BRET (*to* CYRANO): This is madness!

A BUSYBODY (*comes up to* CYRANO): What a scandal! Montfleury, the great actor! He is protected by the Duke de Candale! Have you a sponsor?

CYRANO: No!

THE BUSYBODY: You don't have a . . .

CYRANO: No! I don't rely on some distant person for protection. (*Puts his hand on his sword*) My protector is always near at hand.

THE BUSYBODY: But. . .

CYRANO: Go! Or tell me why you're looking at my nose.

THE BUSYBODY (*frightened*): I. . .

CYRANO: Do you find it surprising?

THE BUSYBODY (*stepping back*): You're mistaken, my lord. . .

CYRANO: Does it disgust you?

THE BUSYBODY: Not at all.

CYRANO: Then why the sneering look? Maybe you find it a little too large?

THE BUSYBODY (*stammering*): Oh, no, it's quite small. . . tiny. . .

CYRANO: What? You accuse me of being an idiot? My nose small? My nose is *huge!* You cruel, flat-nosed fool! I carry it with pride. A big nose is a sign of kindness, courtesy, wit, and courage. I have all those qualities. You can never hope to have any of them. (*Slaps him. Then turns him around and kicks him in the seat of his pants.*)

THE BUSYBODY (*running away*): Help, guards!

CYRANO: Let that be a lesson to anyone else who may feel that the middle of my face is amusing.

DE GUICHE (*who has come down from the seats*): He's beginning to annoy me. Isn't anyone going to stand up to him?

VALVERT: Yes, *I* will. Watch! (*Walks up to* CYRANO) You have a very—ah—large nose.

CYRANO (*seriously*): Yes, very. Is that all?

VALVERT: Well. . .

CYRANO: I'm afraid your speech was a bit short. You might have said all sorts of things, changing your tone to fit your words. For example:
Aggressive: "If I had a nose like that, I'd have it amputated!"
Friendly: "The end of it must get wet when you drink from a cup. Why don't you use a goblet?"

Curious: "What do you use it for? Do you keep your pens and scissors in it?"
Gracious: "What a kind man you are! You love birds so much, you've given them a perch to rest on.
Thoughtful: "You should have an awning put over it to protect it from the sun."
Dramatic: "When it bleeds, it must be like the Red Sea!" There, you have an idea of what you might have said to me if you were witty and a man of letters. But you are a man of few letters: only the four that spell "fool."

DE GUICHE (*trying to lead away the outraged* VALVERT): Come, what nonsense.

VALVERT: Such arrogant airs! From a country bumpkin who—who—doesn't even wear gloves!

CYRANO: I have no gloves? It doesn't bother me. I had a pair, but lost one of them. So I threw the other away—in someone's face.

VALVERT: Jerk!

CYRANO (*taking off his hat and bowing, as if* VALVERT *had just introduced himself*): Delighted to meet you. I'm Cyrano de Bergerac.

VALVERT (*annoyed*): Buffoon!

CYRANO (*drawing his sword*): Oh! I have a tingling in my sword.

VALVERT (*drawing his own*): So be it!

CYRANO: I'll give you a charming little thrust.

VALVERT (*with scorn*): Poet!

CYRANO: Yes, I am. And I will show you by composing a poem while I fence with you. And when I come to the last line, I'll draw blood.

VALVERT: No!

CYRANO: Oh, yes. "Poem of the Duel between Mr. de Bergerac and an Idiot at the Hôtel de Bourgogne."

VALVERT: What's that?

CYRANO: That's the title.

THE CROWD (*excited*): Make room! No noise.

(*They begin to fence.* CYRANO's *actions match his words. He recites a poem. When he finishes the last line, he thrusts his sword at* VALVERT. VALVERT *staggers,* CYRANO *bows. There are great cheers from the crowd. Officers surround* CYRANO *and congratulate him.* VALVERT's *friends hold him up and lead him away.*)

THE CROWD (*surrounding* CYRANO): Bravo!

LE BRET (*to* CYRANO): I'd like to talk to you.

CYRANO: Wait until the crowd goes away. (*To* BELLEROSE) May I remain?

BELLEROSE: Of course! (*To the* DOORKEEPER) Clear the theater, but leave the candles burning. We'll come back after dinner to rehearse a new play for tomorrow.

(BELLEROSE *and* JODELET *bow and exit.*)

THE DOORKEEPER (*to* CYRANO): Aren't you going to dine?

CYRANO: No.

(*The* DOORKEEPER *withdraws.*)

LE BRET (*to* CYRANO): Why not?

CYRANO: Because I have no money.

LE BRET: What? That bag of money. . .

CYRANO: Alas, my month's allowance gone in a single day!

LE BRET: And for the rest of the month?

CYRANO: I have nothing left.

LE BRET: How foolish to throw it all away!

CYRANO: But what a gesture.

THE ORANGE GIRL (*from behind her counter*): Sir, to know you're fasting breaks my heart. I have plenty. (*Points to the refreshment table*) Take what you like.

CYRANO: My child, my Gascon pride forbids me to accept a bit of food. But since I don't want to offend you, I will accept. (*He goes to the refreshment table. He chooses one grape, a glass of water, and half a macaroon.*)

LE BRET: That's ridiculous.

THE ORANGE GIRL: Please, something more.

CYRANO: Yes. Your hand to kiss.

(*He kisses her hand as if it were that of a princess.*)

THE ORANGE GIRL: Thank you, sir. Good evening. (*She bows and leaves.*)

# Scene 4

*The theater in the Hôtel de Bourgogne.* CYRANO, LE BRET, *the* DOORKEEPER, *and the* CHAPERON.

CYRANO (*sets the macaroon down on the table in front of him*): My dinner! (*Sets down the glass of water*) My drink! (*Sets down the grape*) My dessert! I'm quite hungry. But first, what is it you wanted to talk to me about?

LE BRET: You're going to have some badly twisted ideas if you keep listening to those warlike fools. Speak with more sensible people, and you'll learn to control your sudden bursts of emotion.

CYRANO (*finishing his macaroon*): It was huge!

LE BRET: You've made too many enemies.

CYRANO: How many would you say I made this evening?

LE BRET: Forty-eight. Not counting the women.

CYRANO (*beginning to eat his grape*): That many?

LE BRET: Cyrano, where will your life lead you? What is your plan?

CYRANO: Once, I was confused by all the choices open to me. Finally, I chose—

LE BRET: What?

CYRANO: The most simple choice of all. I decided to be admired in everything—by everyone!

LE BRET (*shrugging*): If you say so. But tell me something. What is the real reason behind your hatred of Montfleury?

CYRANO: That fat, old fool. His stomach is so big he can't even see his feet. Yet, he still thinks of himself as a ladies' man. I've hated him since I saw him glance one evening at her—

LE BRET (*shocked*): What? Can it be possible. . . ?

CYRANO (*laughs bitterly*): That I'm in love? (*Changes to a serious tone*) It's true.

LE BRET: With whom? You've never told me.

CYRANO: Think a moment. This nose of mine precedes me by a quarter of an hour wherever I go. It stops me from dreaming of being loved by even an ugly woman. So whom else would I love but the most beautiful woman in the world?

LE BRET: The most beautiful. . .

CYRANO: Of course! The most charming. . . the most intelligent. . . the fairest. . .

LE BRET: For heaven's sake, who is she?

CYRANO: She's a mortal danger without trying to be one. She's a trap set by nature. She's a rose in which love hides in ambush! Neither the great beauties Venus nor Diana can compare to her when she goes through the Paris streets.

LE BRET: *Now*, it is becoming clear. Your cousin, Roxane?

CYRANO: Yes—Roxane.

LE BRET: Then you should be thrilled. Tell her

you love her. You covered yourself with glory in her eyes today.

CYRANO: Look at me. Tell me what hope this monstrous nose might leave me! I don't allow myself any illusions. Sometimes, I go into a garden and see a man and woman strolling together in the moonlight. I think of how I, too, would like to walk arm in arm with a woman under the moon. Then I suddenly notice the shadow of my nose on the garden wall!

LE BRET (*deeply moved*): My friend. . .

CYRANO: I have unhappy hours when I feel that I am so ugly, and sometimes all alone. . .

LE BRET (*concerned, taking his hand*): You weep?

CYRANO: No, never! It would be too ugly if a tear should roll down this nose!

LE BRET: Come, don't be sad. Love is but a game of chance! Look at the girl who offered you the food just now. You could plainly see that she did not detest you.

CYRANO (*impressed*): Yes, that is true!

LE BRET: And Roxane herself turned pale as she watched your duel!

CYRANO: Pale?

LE BRET: Her heart and mind are already moved to wonder. Speak to her, tell her. . .

CYRANO: So that she will laugh at my nose? No! That is the only thing in the world I fear.

(*The* DOORKEEPER *enters and brings in* ROXANE'*s* CHAPERON.)

DOORKEEPER: Sir, someone is asking for you—

CYRANO (*seeing the* CHAPERON): Ah, Heavens, her chaperon!

CHAPERON (*bowing low*): My lady wishes me to ask her brave cousin where she can meet him privately.

CYRANO (*amazed*): Meet me?

CHAPERON (*bowing again*): Yes. She has something to tell you.

CYRANO (*staggering*): Oh, my God!

CHAPERON: She will go to early mass tomorrow morning at Saint Roch church. Is there a place nearby to meet afterward?

CYRANO (*carried away*): Where? I—but—Oh! my God! I am trying to think. At—at Ragueneau's—the pastry cook's.

CHAPERON (*leaving*): Be there at seven o'clock.

CYRANO: I will be there.

(*The* CHAPERON *exits.*)

# Scene 5

*The theater in the Hôtel de Bourgogne.* CYRANO *and* LE BRET.

CYRANO (*falling into* LE BRET'*s arms*): Me! She wants to see *me!*

LE BRET: I see your sadness has vanished. But please be calm.

(CUIGY, BRISSAILLE, *and several officers enter.*
*They are holding up* LIGNIÈRE.)

CYRANO: Lignière! What's happened to you?

BRISSAILLE: He is afraid. He can't go home.

CYRANO: Why not?

LIGNIÈRE: A note warns me a hundred men will
attack me at Port de Nesle on my way
home. Can I stay with you tonight?

CYRANO: A hundred men you say? You shall
sleep in your own house.

LIGNIÈRE (*alarmed*): But. . .

CYRANO (*in a loud voice*): Take that lantern and
walk. I'll cover you. (*To the officers*) And
you. . . follow at a distance and be witnesses.
When you see me charge, don't come to
help me. No matter what the danger may
be. (*To the violinists*) You shall play a tune
as we march. (*A large group forms, consisting
of actors, actresses, officers, musicians.
Lighted candles are handed out. It becomes a
torchlight march.*) Doorkeeper, open the
door!

ALL: To the Porte de Nesle!

(CYRANO *goes out. The group follows. The curtain
falls.*)

**21**

# ACT 2

**The Poet's Cook Shop**

*This act takes place in the shop of Ragueneau, baker and pastry cook. Cyrano comes early one morning to meet his cousin Roxane, the woman he secretly loves. Roxane confesses to him that she is secretly in love with someone. At first, Cyrano's hopes rise when he believes she's in love with him. But Roxane names the young newcomer, Christian de Neuvillette, as the object of her love.*

*Christian has joined the Gascony Guards, the regiment that Cyrano belongs to. Roxane asks him to promise to protect Christian from harm, and he agrees. Cyrano and Christian meet. Then Cyrano comes up with a plan. It will allow Christian to impress Roxane. At the same time, it will satisfy Cyrano's own need to express his love for Roxane.*

## Scene 1

*The pastry shop.* RAGUENEAU *and* PASTRY COOKS *enter.*

FIRST PASTRY COOK (*with a plate*): Puff paste!

SECOND PASTRY COOK (*with a dish*): And candied fruits!

THIRD PASTRY COOK (*with a pan*): Filet of beef with sauce!

RAGUENEAU (*looking up*): There's something missing in this sauce.

PASTRY COOK: What shall I do to it?

RAGUENEAU: Make it more poetic!

AN ASSISTANT COOK: I've baked this in your honor, sir! (*He uncovers a tray revealing a large pastry lyre.*)

RAGUENEAU (*thrilled*): A lyre! (*Giving him some money*) Here, go and drink to my health. (LISE *enters.*) My wife! (*To* LISE, *pointing at the lyre*) Isn't it beautiful?

LISE (*puts a pile of paper bags on the counter and looks at the lyre*): Absurd!

RAGUENEAU: Bags? But these are made from my treasured books. . . the poetry of my friends.

LISE (*angrily*): I have a right to make use of the only thing they leave for payment. .

RAGUENEAU: How can you treat poetry with such disrespect?

LISE: There was nothing else to do with them.

RAGUENEAU: What would you have done to essays?

(CYRANO *enters.*)

CYRANO: What time is it?

RAGUENEAU: Six o'clock.

CYRANO (*with great emotion*): One more hour! (*Begins to pace back and forth*) I'm waiting for someone to arrive. When she does, I want you to leave us alone together.

RAGUENEAU: I can't. My poets will soon be here.

LISE (*sarcastically*): For their first meal!

CYRANO: You will take them away when I give

you a signal. (*He sits down at* Ragueneau's *table and takes a sheet of paper.*) A pen?

Ragueneau (*offering him one from behind his ear*): A swan's quill!

Cyrano (*takes his pen, waves* Ragueneau *away, and says to himself*): Write a note. . . fold it. . . give it to her. . . run away. You don't have the courage to say one word to her! (*To* Ragueneau) What time is it?

Ragueneau: A quarter past six.

Cyrano: I'm afraid to say aloud the feelings I have in here. (*Strikes his chest*) But writing is a different matter. (*Takes his pen again*) I have only to look into my soul and copy the words inscribed in it.

(*He begins to write. Through the glass door, thin figures are seen moving hesitantly.*)

# Scene 2

*The pastry shop.* Poets, *dressed in muddy black clothes, enter.*

Lise: Here are your poets, covered in mud.

First Poet (*to* Ragueneau): Colleague.

Second Poet (*shaking hands*): Honored colleague!

Third Poet (*sniffs*): It smells good in here.

Ragueneau (*surrounded, embraced*): How quickly one feels at ease with them!

First Poet: We were delayed by the crowd at the Porte de Nesle.

SECOND POET: Eight bandits, ripped open by the sword, lay bleeding on the pavement.

CYRANO (*lifting his head a moment*): Eight? I thought it was seven. (*Returns to his letter*)

RAGUENEAU (*to* CYRANO): Do you know the hero of the combat?

CYRANO (*carelessly*): Me? No?

FIRST POET: We were told that a man alone had routed the whole band. The man who could do a thing like that must be a terrible giant.

CYRANO (*writing and reading to himself*): "Your lips. . ."

SECOND POET (*grabbing a cake*): What have you been writing, Ragueneau?

CYRANO: "Your faithful worshiper. . ." (*He stops as he is about to sign his name. He stands up and puts the letter in his pocket.*) No need to sign it. I shall give it to her myself.

RAGUENEAU (*to the* SECOND POET): I've written a recipe in verse.

THIRD POET (*sitting down next to a platter of cream puffs*): Give us the poem!

(RAGUENEAU *clears his throat, straightens his hat, and strikes a pose. He recites his poem.*)

THE POETS (*with their mouths full*): Charming! Delightful!

(*They retire into the background, still eating.* CYRANO, *who has been watching, comes up to* RAGUENEAU.)

CYRANO: Don't you see how they stuff themselves?

RAGUENEAU: Of course, but I don't want to embarrass them. To repeat my verses to them gives me double pleasure. I satisfy myself and feed those who might go hungry.

CYRANO: Oh, you please me. (RAGUENEAU *goes to rejoin his friends.* ROXANE, *masked, appears behind the glass of the front door, followed by the* CHAPERON. CYRANO *motions* RAGUENEAU *to take the* POETS *away.*)

RAGUENEAU (*showing the* POETS *another door on the right*): Come this way, gentlemen. We'll be more comfortable in there.

(*They exit, after having grabbed several trays of pastry.*)

CYRANO: I'll give her my letter if there's the least hope. (*He opens the door.*) Come in! (*Takes the* CHAPERON *aside*) May I have a word with you? (CYRANO *speaks with* the CHAPERON. *He offers her bags filled with pastry. She accepts them.*) I'm sure you'll enjoy eating this on the street. (*Pushes her outside*) Please don't return until you've finished. (*He closes the door and comes back to* ROXANE.) Now, let this moment be blessed above all others: the day when you remembered my existence and came here to tell me. . . to tell me?

ROXANE (*unmasked*): I wanted to tell you. But before I make my confession, let me see you again as I did in the past when we would play together.

CYRANO: Yes—you came every year to Bergerac.

ROXANE: We played all sorts of games. Sometimes, you came running with your hand bloody from climbing. (*She takes his hand and stops in surprise.*) Oh, even now, you've done it again. You're still hurting yourself. How did you do it this time?

CYRANO: I was *playing* again—at Porte de Nesle.

ROXANE: How many were there against you?

CYRANO: Oh, not quite a hundred.

ROXANE: Tell me about it.

CYRANO: No—let it pass. Tell me what it is you were afraid to speak of just now.

ROXANE: I'm in love with someone.

CYRANO: Ah!

ROXANE: Someone who doesn't know.

CYRANO: Ah!

ROXANE: A poor fellow who until now has loved me from far off. He hasn't dared say anything.

CYRANO: Ah!

ROXANE: As it happens, cousin, he serves in your regiment. In fact, he's a cadet in your company.

CYRANO: Ah!

ROXANE: His face glows with wit, with genius; he is proud, young, fearless, handsome—

CYRANO (*rising, very pale*): Handsome!

ROXANE: What's the matter?

CYRANO: With me? Nothing—It is—it is—

ROXANE: Well, I love him, even though I have never seen him except at the theater.

CYRANO: You have never spoken with him?

ROXANE: Only with our eyes.

CYRANO: Then how do you know he loves you?

ROXANE: People gossip. Friends have told me.

CYRANO: His name?

ROXANE: The Baron Christian de Neuvillette. He began to serve this morning.

CYRANO: You've lost your heart so quickly! But my poor girl, you're so fond of fine speech and wit. What if he should prove to be unlearned or a fool.

ROXANE (*stamping her foot*): Well, then I'll die!

CYRANO: You brought me here to tell me this? I don't understand why.

ROXANE: Yesterday, someone broke my heart. I was told that everyone in your company is a Gascon—

CYRANO: And we challenge any newcomer who is admitted without being a Gascon.

ROXANE: Yes! You can imagine how I feared for him when I heard it. But I saw you yesterday holding all those brutes at bay. I said to myself, "Everyone fears him. If he were willing to. . ."

CYRANO: Very well. I'll protect your little baron.

ROXANE: You'll be his friend?

CYRANO: I will.

ROXANE: And he'll never have a duel?

CYRANO: No. I promise.

ROXANE: Oh! I love you. Now I must go. (*Quickly puts on her mask and speaks absent-mindedly*) But you haven't told me about your battle last night. Tell him to write me. Oh, I love you.

CYRANO: Yes, yes.

ROXANE: A hundred men! What courage!

CYRANO (*bowing*): Oh, I've done better since then.

(*She leaves.* CYRANO *remains motionless, looking down at the floor.*)

# Scene 3

*The pastry shop.* RAGUENEAU *enters.*

RAGUENEAU: May we come back in?

CYRANO (*without moving*): Yes.

(RAGUENEAU *signals to his friends, and they come in. At the same time, Captain* CARBON DE CASTEL-JALOUX *appears at the door in the background. He makes broad gestures when he sees* CYRANO.)

CARBON: There he is!

CYRANO (*looking up*): Captain!

CARBON: Our hero! We know all about it. Thirty of my cadets are here. Here they come!

(Cadets *enter.*)

Several Cadets: Let's all embrace him.

Cyrano: Please, please. . .

Le Bret (*entering and hurrying to* Cyrano): They are looking for you! A wild crowd led by those who marched after you last night. (*In a low voice, smiling at* Cyrano.) Did you see Roxane?

Cyrano (*sharply*): Hush!

The Crowd (*shouting from outside*): Cyrano!

(*A mob bursts into the pastry shop. Cheers and shouting.*)

Ragueneau (*standing on a table*): In they come. They're breaking everything. It's wonderful!

A Young Marquis (*rushing toward* Cyrano *with outstretched hands*): If you only knew, my dear Cyrano. . .

Cyrano: Your dear Cyrano? How can I be your dear Cyrano? I've never seen you before.

Another Marquis: I wish to present you, sir, to some ladies there in my carriage.

Cyrano (*coldly*): And who will introduce me to you?

Le Bret (*surprised*): What's the matter with you?

Cyrano: Quiet! Enough!

(The Crowd *moves. The people step aside.* De Guiche *appears, escorted by* Officers. *Then* Cuigy, Brissaille, *and more* Officers *enter.* Cuigy *hurries to* Cyrano.)

CUIGY (*to* CYRANO): Mr. de Guiche comes on behalf of Marshal de Gassion! (*Everyone steps aside.*)

DE GUICHE (*bowing to* CYRANO): The marshal has learned of your latest exploit. He wishes to express his admiration to you.

CYRANO (*bowing*): The marshal well knows what bravery is.

DE GUICHE: Your career is already rich in fine exploits. You serve among the Gascons, no?

CYRANO: In the cadets, yes.

DE GUICHE: And a poet, too. Would you like to become one of my followers?

CYRANO: No, sir, I prefer to follow no one.

DE GUICHE: You're a proud man.

CYRANO: Really, you have noticed it?

(*A* CADET *enters. He's holding his sword overhead. It's strung with hats, their feathers drooping. The hats are knocked in and full of holes.*)

CADET: Look, Cyrano, at the strange feathered game we took in the street this morning! The hats of those you routed. (*Everyone laughs.*)

CUIGY: The man who hired them must be in a rage today.

BRISSAILLE: Does any one know who it was?

DE GUICHE: It was me. (*The laughter stops.*) I

hired them to punish a drunken poet.

CADET (*pointing to the hats*): What shall we do with these? Make them into a stew?

CYRANO (*takes the sword upon which they are strung. He salutes and lets them slide off at* DE GUICHE's *feet.*): Sir, will you return these to your friends?

DE GUICHE (*stands up suddenly*): Bring my sedan chair at once. I must go. (*To* CYRANO, *angrily*) You, sir! (*Regaining his self-control, smiling*) Have you read *Don Quixote?*

CYRANO: Yes, and at that scatterbrain's name, I take off my hat.

DE GUICHE: You would do well to think of the chapter on windmills. Because when one attacks them, their great arms often hurl you into the mud.

CYRANO: Or up to the stars.

(DE GUICHE *leaves, carried off on his chair. The* OFFICERS *walk away, whispering. The* CROWD *leaves.*)

# Scene 4

*The pastry shop. The* CADETs *are seated at tables and are being served food and drink.*

LE BRET (*throwing up his arms in despair*): What a misfortune!

CYRANO: Oh! You grumbler!

LE BRET: If you would lay aside your proud

spirit a little, fortune and glory could be yours.

CYRANO: And what must I do? Seek some protector, get a powerful patron? Dedicate poems to bankers, as others do? No, thank you. I prefer to lead a different kind of life. I sing, dream, laugh, and go where I please, alone and free. I dream of flying to the moon, but give no thought to fame or fortune. I may not rise very high, but I'll climb alone.

LE BRET: Alone, so be it. But not one against all!

CYRANO: Well, yes. It is my weakness. It pleases me to displease. I love to be hated.

LE BRET: Proclaim your pride and bitterness to the world. But softly tell me that she doesn't love you.

CYRANO (*sharply*): Hush!

(*After a moment,* CHRISTIAN *enters and joins the* CADETS. *They don't speak to him. He sits down at a small table, where* LISE *waits on him.*)

FIRST CADET: Cyrano! Will you tell us your story now?

CYRANO (*looks around*): Not now. A little later.

(*He and* LE BRET *walk off talking quietly together.*)

FIRST CADET (*rising*): The story of Cyrano's fight will be the best lesson for this untried recruit. (*Stops at* CHRISTIAN'*s table*)

CHRISTIAN (*looking up*): Untried recruit?

FIRST CADET: Mr. de Neuvillette, it's time for you to learn something. There is one object we do not mention—any more than we would mention rope in the house of a hanged man.

CHRISTIAN: What is it?

SECOND CADET: Look at me! (*Puts his finger to his nose three times*) Do you understand?

CHRISTIAN: I think so. You must mean. . .

THIRD CADET: Sh! You must never speak that word. (*Points to* CYRANO) Or you will have to answer to him over there.

(CHRISTIAN *gets up and walks over to Captain* CARBON DE CASTEL-JALOUX.)

CHRISTIAN: Captain, what should one do when southerners are too boastful?

CARBON: Prove to them that a northerner can be brave.

CHRISTIAN: Thank you.

FIRST CADET (*to* CYRANO): Now tell us your story!

CYRANO (*comes toward them*): My story? Well, I was walking alone to meet them. The sky was pitch black. There were no lights in the street. I couldn't see . . .

CHRISTIAN: Beyond the end of your nose.

(*Silence. The* CADETS *look at* CYRANO *in terror.*)

CYRANO: Who is this?

FIRST CADET: He came to us this morning.

CYRANO (*stepping toward* CHRISTIAN): This morning?

CARBON (*softly*): His name is Christian de Neuvil—

CYRANO: Ah! Very well. (*Turns pale, then angry. Makes a movement as if to attack* CHRISTIAN. *Then calms himself.*) Well—as I was saying. I walked on. I thought that for the sake of a poor drunkard, I was about to offend some mighty prince who would. . .

(*The* CADETS *stand up.* CHRISTIAN *tilts his chair.*)

CHRISTIAN: Resent your nosiness.

CYRANO (*choking*): . . . hold a grudge against me, and that I was putting. . .

CHRISTIAN: Your nose into. . .

CYRANO (*exploding*): Out! All of you. Get out!

(*The* CADETS *rush toward the doors.*)

FIRST CADET: The tiger has finally awakened.

CYRANO: Leave me alone with this man.

SECOND CADET: We'll find him cut into mincemeat!

THIRD CADET: It makes me shake to think of what will happen to him.

(*They all go out, leaving* CYRANO *and* CHRISTIAN *standing face to face.*)

# Scene 5

*The pastry shop.* CYRANO *and* CHRISTIAN *are alone.*

CYRANO: Brave man!

CHRISTIAN: But—

CYRANO: Embrace me; I am her cousin.

CHRISTIAN: Whose?

CYRANO: Roxane's.

CHRISTIAN (*rushing toward him*): You? Her cousin?

CYRANO: Well, yes.

CHRISTIAN: And she's told you—

CYRANO: Everything!

CHRISTIAN: Does she love me?

CYRANO: Perhaps so!

CHRISTIAN (*taking his hands*): How happy I am to know you.

CYRANO: This might be called a sudden friendship. (*Looks closely at him and says to himself*) True, he *is* a handsome rascal!

CHRISTIAN: If you knew, sir, how I admire you!

CYRANO: But all those jokes about my nose—

CHRISTIAN: Forgive me. I take them all back.

CYRANO: Roxane expects a letter tonight.

CHRISTIAN: No! I shall spoil my chances if I speak!

CYRANO: Why?

CHRISTIAN: I am—I know it—a man who cannot talk of love. If only I could speak more gracefully. Roxane is so educated. I shall surely kill all her illusions.

CYRANO: If I only had such a handsome interpreter to speak my soul!

CHRISTIAN (*in despair*): I need eloquence.

CYRANO (*suddenly*): I'll lend you mine! Lend me

your beautiful features, and together we'll form a romantic hero.

CHRISTIAN: What are you talking about?

CYRANO: Roxane will not lose her illusions. Together, we can win her heart. Will you do it?

CHRISTIAN: Will it give you such pleasure?

CYRANO (*happily*): It would. . .amuse me! You will be my good looks, and I your wit.

CHRISTIAN: But I can never write the needed letter. It must be sent without delay!

CYRANO (*taking out the letter he has written*): Here is your letter! It needs only the name and address.

CHRISTIAN: I don't understand.

CYRANO: You can send it as it is. Don't worry.

CHRISTIAN: You had already—

CYRANO: I always have a letter in my pocket, written to some imaginary lady.

CHRISTIAN: Won't some words have to be changed?

CYRANO: It will fit Roxane like a glove! Count on her conceit to make her think it was written for her.

CHRISTIAN: My friend!

(CHRISTIAN *throws himself into* CYRANO's *arms. They embrace.*)

CADETS (*enter and see the men embracing*): What is this?

FIRST CADET (*in a mocking way*): Well, now you can speak to him about his nose. Watch this! (*Approaches* CYRANO *and stares at his nose*) What is that long thing on your face, sir? It reminds me of something, but I can't remember what it is.

CYRANO: Then let me help you! (*Slaps him. The other* CADETS *are thrilled to see* CYRANO *behave like himself again. They dance happily. The curtain falls.*)

# *ACT 3*

**Roxane's Kiss**

*This act takes place in the street under Roxane's balcony. Count de Guiche arrives and declares his love for Roxane. He says that he is going off to war as the commander of Cyrano's and Christian's regiment. Roxane pretends that she has a strong affection for de Guiche so that he will agree not to send the regiment to battle.*

*Christian wishes to end the game he and Cyrano have come up with. He wishes to speak to Roxane in his own words. However, when he tries, he is a terrible failure. Cyrano, hiding under the balcony, has to feed Christian with the right words to satisfy Roxane. Christian and Roxane marry. When de Guiche learns of this, he orders the Gascony Guards to the front.*

## Scene 1

*A street under* ROXANE'S *balcony. As the curtain rises, the* CHAPERON *is seated on a bench. The window is wide open.*

CHAPERON: Roxane! Are you ready?

ROXANE'S VOICE: I am coming.

CYRANO'S VOICE (*singing offstage*)*:* La, la!

CYRANO (*enters, followed by two pages carrying lutes*): Those are thirty-second notes, you fool!

FIRST PAGE: Ah, so you know about thirty-second notes, sir!

CYRANO (*takes the lute away from him*): I'm a musician, too. Let me do it!

ROXANE (*appearing on the balcony*): Ah, it's you. I'm coming down!

CHAPERON: Where did the musicians come from?

CYRANO: I won them on a bet. They have been ordered to play music and follow me for a day. At first, it was delightful, but now not so much so. (*To the pages*) Go play for Montfleury—and play for a long time, out of tune! (*They leave.*) I've come to ask Roxane whether her friend is still perfect.

ROXANE (*coming out of the house*): Oh, Cyrano, how witty and handsome he is. And how I love him.

CYRANO (*smiling*): Christian is so witty? Does he speak well about things of the heart?

ROXANE: Not well—brilliantly.

CYRANO: And how does he write?

ROXANE: Better than he speaks. Listen. "The more you take of my heart, the more I have left." Isn't that wonderful?

CYRANO: Pooh!

ROXANE: And this: "Since I need a heart with which to suffer, if you keep mine, send me yours!"

CYRANO: Sometimes he has too much, sometimes not enough. What does he wish?

ROXANE: You're teasing me! It is jealousy!

CYRANO: What?

ROXANE: You're jealous of the way he writes.

CHAPERON: Mr. de Guiche is coming! (*She pushes* CYRANO *toward the house.*) Go inside. It will be better, perhaps, if he does not find you here; it might make him suspicious—

ROXANE: Yes, of my dear secret! He's in love with me, and he's powerful. He must not know. He might strike a blow at Christian.

CYRANO (*entering the house*): Very well!

(DE GUICHE *appears.*)

DE GUICHE: I have come to say farewell.

ROXANE: Are you going away?

DE GUICHE: To war.

ROXANE: Ah!

DE GUICHE: I have orders. We're besieging Arras.

ROXANE: Ah! A siege?

DE GUICHE: Yes. My going seems to leave you cold.

ROXANE (*politely*): Not at all.

DE GUICHE: I'm in despair. Will I ever see you again? Do you know that I have been named commander?

ROXANE (*uninterested*): Bravo!

DE GUICHE: I'm in command of the guards—of the regiment in which your boastful cousin serves. I shall have my revenge on him at Arras.

ROXANE: What—the guards are being sent there? (*Aside*) Christian!

DE GUICHE: What is the matter?

ROXANE (*emotionally*): This departure fills me with despair. To know the one I care for is off to war!

DE GUICHE (*surprised*): For the first time, on the day I leave, you speak a kind word to me.

ROXANE (*changing her tone*): Your revenge on Cyrano is perhaps to expose him to battle, which he adores. A sorry vengeance! But I know what would be horrible to him.

DE GUICHE: What?

ROXANE: When the regiment goes off to fight, leave him and his cadets behind in Paris. If you wish to punish him, then deprive him of danger.

DE GUICHE: Only a woman could think of such a great trick.

ROXANE: He'll eat his heart out, and you will be avenged.

DE GUICHE: In taking up my grudge, is that a sign that you love me a little?

ROXANE: It is. (*She smiles.*)

DE GUICHE: I will keep the orders for the cadets here. (*Puts them in his pocket. Moves closer.*) You drive me mad! I planned on leaving tonight. But how can I when you just showed me such feelings? Let me stay behind one day. I'll come to you tonight.

ROXANE: I must forbid it.

DE GUICHE: Ah!

ROXANE: Go and be a hero. (*Aside*) And Christian stays.

DE GUICHE: Okay! I am going.

(*He kisses her hand and leaves. The* CHAPERON *returns.*)

ROXANE: Say nothing of what I have just done. Cyrano will be angry with me for robbing him of his war! (*She calls toward the house.*) Cousin! (CYRANO *returns.*) If Christian comes, as I presume he will, let him wait for me.

CYRANO: And what are you going to question him about today?

ROXANE: Nothing. If he knew, he would prepare himself. I'll say "Improvise. Speak to me of love in your own way."

CYRANO (*smiling*): Good.

(CHRISTIAN *approaches.*)

ROXANE: Oh, no! Here he comes! (*She leaves.*)

CYRANO (*calling*): Christian!

# Scene 2

*A street under* ROXANE'S *balcony.* CYRANO *and* CHRISTIAN *stand together.*

CYRANO: I know all about it! Prepare your memory. Here is an opportunity to cover yourself with glory. Don't look so unhappy. Quick, let us return to your house, for I am going to teach you—

CHRISTIAN: No!

CYRANO: What madness has seized you?

CHRISTIAN: I'm sick of borrowing letters and speeches and playing this timid part. It was good at first, but now I feel she loves me! I am not afraid. I'll speak for myself.

CYRANO: Indeed!

CHRISTIAN: Who told you that I should not know how? I am not so stupid. You'll see. (*He sees* ROXANE *coming.*) Here she comes! Wait, Cyrano, don't leave me!

CYRANO: Speak for yourself, sir. (*Disappears behind the garden wall*)

ROXANE: Ah, it's you. Let us sit down. Talk to me. I am listening.

CHRISTIAN: I love you.

ROXANE: Yes, speak to me of love.

CHRISTIAN: I love you.

ROXANE: That's the theme—now embroider it.

CHRISTIAN: I should be so happy if you loved me. Tell me that you do, Roxane.

ROXANE (*pouting*): You're giving me water when I expected wine. Tell me how you love me.

CHRISTIAN: I adore you.

ROXANE (*standing up and moving away*): Oh!

CHRISTIAN: Yes. . . I'm becoming foolish.

ROXANE: And it displeases me as much as if you should become ugly.

**46**

CHRISTIAN: Wait! Let me tell you.

ROXANE (*opening the door*): That you adore me. Yes, I know. Now go away. (*She closes the door in his face.*)

CYRANO (*who has returned without being seen*): It is a success?

CHRISTIAN: It is a disaster! Help me!

CYRANO: How the devil can I teach you on the spot?

CHRISTIAN (*gripping his arm*): Oh, come now, see!

(*The window of the balcony is lighted up.*)

CYRANO (*with emotion*): Her window!

CHRISTIAN: I shall die!

CYRANO: Hush! Stand there, in front of the balcony. I will take my place underneath and whisper words to you.

CHRISTIAN: But—

CYRANO: Now call her!

CHRISTIAN: Roxane!

CYRANO (*picks up some pebbles*): Wait until I throw a pebble at the window.

ROXANE (*opening the window*): Who's there?

CHRISTIAN: Christian.

ROXANE (*with disdain*): Is it you?

CHRISTIAN: I wish to speak with you.

ROXANE: No, your speech is too awkward. Go away!

CHRISTIAN: Forgive me!

ROXANE: No, you no longer love me!

CHRISTIAN (*repeating* CYRANO'S *words*): What a charge! That I love you no longer—when I love you so much more.

ROXANE (*stopping, as she was about to close the window*): That's better!

CHRISTIAN (*still repeating*): Love grows. . . rocked in my restless soul. . . which this cruel boy takes for his cradle!

ROXANE: Very good. But why are you hesitating?

CYRANO (*pulling* CHRISTIAN *under the balcony and taking his place*): Hush! This is becoming too hard.

ROXANE: Today, your words are faltering. Why?

CYRANO (*speaking softly, like* CHRISTIAN): Because of the darkness, they must grope to find your ears.

ROXANE: They seem to be climbing better now.

CYRANO: They have gotten used to the exercise.

ROXANE (*making a movement*): I'm coming down.

CYRANO (*quickly*): No!

ROXANE: Why not?

CYRANO: Let us take advantage of this chance to speak together without seeing each other.

ROXANE: Why?

CYRANO: I find it delightful. You see the blackness of a long cloak. I see the whiteness of a summer dress. I'm only a shadow. You're only a gleam of light.

ROXANE: You've never talked to me like this before. What else will you say to me?

CYRANO: All the words that come to me. I will throw them at you wildly, rather than arranging them in a bouquet: I love you, I love you madly.

ROXANE (*her voice shaking*): Yes, this is really love. I am trembling, and I am weeping. I love you, and I am yours. I'm drunk with love!

CYRANO: Then let death come! I ask only one thing.

CHRISTIAN (*from under the balcony*): A kiss!

ROXANE (*quickly drawing back*): What?

CYRANO (*in a low voice to* CHRISTIAN): You're moving too fast! (*To* ROXANE) I asked for a kiss. But I realize that I was too bold.

ROXANE (*a little disappointed*): You don't insist?

CYRANO: I have offended your modesty. Don't give me that kiss.

CHRISTIAN (*to* CYRANO, *pulling his cloak*): Why?

CYRANO: Hush, Christian!

ROXANE (*leaning forward*): What are you saying?

CYRANO: I was scolding myself for having gone too far. (*He hears a noise.*) Wait! Someone's coming!

(ROXANE *closes the window.*)

# Scene 3

*A street under* ROXANE'S *balcony. A* MONK *enters. He has a lantern in his hand, and he goes from house to house.* CYRANO *and* CHRISTIAN *greet him.*

CYRANO (*to the* MONK): What are you doing?

MONK: I'm looking for the home of Madame Madeleine Robin.

CYRANO (*showing him a street leading away from the house*): It's that way—straight ahead.

MONK: Thank you. (*He leaves.*)

CYRANO: Good luck! (*Returns to* CHRISTIAN)

CHRISTIAN: Get me that kiss!

CYRANO: No!

CHRISTIAN: Sooner or later—

(*The balcony window opens again.* CHRISTIAN *hides under the balcony.*)

ROXANE (*coming onto the balcony*): Is it you? We were speaking about—about—a. . .

CYRANO: A kiss. The word is sweet. I do not see why your lips should not try it. If the word burns them now, what will the act do?

ROXANE: Be still!

CYRANO: A kiss, when all is told, what is it? An oath taken directly. A greeting like the sweet breath of a flower. A way of tasting a little of the soul with the edge of the lips.

ROXANE: Come and give me that matchless flower!

CYRANO (*pushing* CHRISTIAN *up*): Climb up to her!

CHRISTIAN (*hesitating*): Now it seems to me that it is wrong.

CYRANO (*pushing him*): Climb, you fool!

(CHRISTIAN *stands on the bench and climbs up.*)

CHRISTIAN: Ah, Roxane! (*Embraces and kisses her*)

CYRANO (*aside*): What a strange pain in my chest! I feel something of that kiss in my heart. Roxane is not only kissing his lips, but also the words I spoke to her. (*He takes a few steps and pretends to have just arrived.*) Roxane!

ROXANE: Who is it?

CYRANO: It is Cyrano. I was passing by. Is Christian still there?

CHRISTIAN (*surprised*): Cyrano!

ROXANE: Good evening, cousin. I'm coming down.

(*She disappears into the house. The* MONK *enters in the background.*)

CHRISTIAN (*sees him*): Not him again!

MONK: It is here! Madeleine Robin's house.

ROXANE (*appears in the doorway*): Who are you?

MONK: I have a letter for you.

CHRISTIAN: A letter?

ROXANE (*opening it*): It's from de Guiche.

CHRISTIAN: He dares?

(ROXANE *reads the letter to herself. It informs her that* DE GUICHE *has stayed behind in a convent while his regiment is preparing to leave. He plans to visit her that night. He sent the letter with a slow-witted monk who would never guess his plan. She then turns to* the MONK.)

ROXANE: Father, you must hear what the letter says. (*Everyone draws near as she pretends to read the letter to them.*)
"The cardinal's wishes must be carried out, however hard it may be for you. Christian must secretly become your husband. I have already sent him to you. I know you dislike him. The monk will give you the blessing of holy matrimony. Resign yourself. You must accept the cardinal's decision."

ROXANE (*to* CHRISTIAN, *in a low voice*): I read letters well, don't I? (*Out loud, with despair*) Oh, this is horrible.

MONK: Resign yourself!

ROXANE: Oh! I am resigned. (*The* MONK *and* CHRISTIAN *enter the house.* ROXANE *speaks softly to* CYRANO.) Count de Guiche will soon arrive. Keep him out! Don't let him come in the house as long as—

CYRANO: I understand. (*To the* MONK) How long will it take to bless them?

MONK: A quarter of an hour.

CYRANO: Hurry, I'll stay here.

(*The door closes.*)

# Scene 4

*A street under* ROXANE'S *balcony.* CYRANO *stands alone.*

CYRANO: How can I detain de Guiche for a quarter of an hour? (*He jumps on the bench and climbs the wall toward the balcony.*) There, I have a plan! Aha, a man is coming!

(*He pulls his hat down over his eyes. Then he takes off his sword, wraps his cloak around him, leans over, and looks down.* DE GUICHE *enters wearing a mask, feeling his way in the darkness. He looks up at* ROXANE'S *house.*)

DE GUICHE: Yes, here it is. I don't see so well. This mask annoys me.

(CYRANO *leaps from the balcony. He lands in between* DE GUICHE *and the front door. He lies on the ground, as if stunned.*)

DE GUICHE (*jumps backward*): What! Where did this man fall from?

CYRANO (*sits up, disguises his voice*): From the moon. What time is it? What country is this? What day? What season?

DE GUICHE: He's lost his reason.

CYRANO: I am dazed. I fell like a bomb from the moon.

DE GUICHE (*out of patience*): Look, sir. . .

CYRANO (*loudly, standing up*): I fell from it!

DE GUICHE: Yes, very well. (*Aside*) Perhaps he is a madman.

CYRANO (*standing in his way*): Where am I? Tell me frankly.

DE GUICHE: Enough of this!

CYRANO (*with a cry of terror*): Oh! My Lord. I believe the people I see in this country have strange faces.

DE GUICHE: What? (*Putting his hand to face*) I'm wearing a mask. (*Trying to get past him*) A lady is expecting me.

CYRANO: Then I must be in Paris, a city of love.

DE GUICHE (*smiling in spite of himself*): He's an amusing fellow.

CYRANO: You're laughing.

DE GUICHE: Yes, but I still wish to pass! I insist—

CYRANO: I catch your meaning!

DE GUICHE: Sir!

CYRANO: You wish to learn from my own lips how the moon is made, and if anyone lives there? Right?

DE GUICHE: No! No! I wish—

CYRANO: To know how I got there? It was by a means of my own invention.

DE GUICHE (*discouraged*): He is mad!

CYRANO (*making a sound of waves, with great mysterious gestures*): Hoo! Hoo!

DE GUICHE: Well?

CYRANO: Can't you guess?

DE GUICHE: No!

CYRANO: The sea! At the time that the tide was attracted by the moon, I lay on the sand. Then I was lifted, headfirst, into the air. I was rising straight up, softly, without effort, like an angel. Suddenly, I felt a shock! Then. . .

DE GUICHE (*suddenly very curious*): Then?

CYRANO (*resumes his natural voice*): Then a quarter of an hour passed, and I let you go. The marriage is over.

DE GUICHE (*leaping to his feet*): I must be dreaming. That voice! (*The door of the house opens, and some light shines through, lighting the street.* CYRANO *removes his hat.*) That nose! Cyrano!

CYRANO (*bowing*): Yes, it is Cyrano. They've just exchanged rings.

DE GUICHE: Who? (*He turns around to see.*)

# Scene 5

*A street under* ROXANE'S *balcony.* CHRISTIAN *and* ROXANE *appear, holding hands. The* MONK *follows them, smiling.*

DE GUICHE: Heavens! You! (*Looking at* ROXANE *and* CHRISTIAN) And he? (*To* ROXANE) Will you say farewell, madame, to your husband?

ROXANE: Why?

DE GUICHE (*to* CHRISTIAN): The regiment is already on the way. Join it!

ROXANE: To go to war?

DE GUICHE: Of course!

ROXANE: But, sir, the cadets are not going.

DE GUICHE: Yes, they are. (*Taking the envelope out of his pocket.*) Here is the order. (*To* CHRISTIAN) Take it, Baron!

ROXANE (*throwing herself in* CHRISTIAN's *arms*): Christian!

DE GUICHE (*sneering, to* CYRANO): The wedding night is still far off!

CYRANO (*aside*): He thinks that causes me great pain!

CHRISTIAN (*to* ROXANE): Your lips again!

CYRANO: Come, come. Enough!

CHRISTIAN: It is hard to leave her. You do not know.

CYRANO (*trying to lead him away*): I do know. . .

(*Drums are heard beating in the distance.*)

DE GUICHE: The regiment is leaving.

ROXANE (*to* CYRANO *as he leads* CHRISTIAN *away*): I trust him to you. Promise me that nothing shall endanger his life.

CYRANO: I shall try, but. . .

ROXANE: Promise me that he will be faithful!

CYRANO: Yes, of course. But—

ROXANE: Promise me that he shall write often!

CYRANO (*stopping*): That, I can promise you!

(*The curtain falls.*)

# ACT 4
## The Gascon Cadets

*This act takes place at the camp of the Gascony Guards at the siege of Arras. The soldiers are suffering from starvation. Roxane arrives by coach with Ragueneau. She brings with her a full supply of food and drink for the soldiers.*

*Christian learns that Roxane is really in love with Cyrano, although she doesn't realize it. Christian demands that Cyrano tell Roxane the truth about the arrangement they have had. Cyrano is about to do just that when the Spanish attack the camp.*

## Scene 1

*The camp of the Gascony Guards. Day is about to dawn. Sentries are stationed to guard against danger. Campfires are burning. The* CADETS, *including* CHRISTIAN, *are asleep.* CARBON *and* LE BRET *are awake.*

LE BRET: It's frightful!

CARBON: Yes.

LE BRET: What a famine!

A SENTRY (*offstage*): Halt! Who goes there?

CYRANO'S VOICE: Bergerac!

LE BRET (*goes to meet* CYRANO): Thank God you're back! Are you wounded?

CYRANO: You know very well they have a habit of missing me every morning.

LE BRET: It is rather foolish to risk your life each day just to carry a letter.

CYRANO: I promised he would write often.

LE BRET: Someday, you should bring back some food for us. We are besieging Arras; yet we are starving!

CYRANO: I must travel light to pass through safely!

LE BRET: To think that every day you risk a life like yours to carry. . . (*Sees* CYRANO *walking toward a tent*) Where are you going?

CYRANO: I am going to write another.

(*A cannon shot is heard, followed immediately by a ruffle of drums.*)

CARBON (*with a sigh*): Reveille! Alas.

First CADET (*sitting up*): I'm hungry!

SECOND CADET: I'm dying of hunger.

ALL: Oh!

CARBON: Get up!

FIRST CADET (*looking in the distance*): Here comes Mr. de Guiche. (*The* CADETS *grumble.*)

CYRANO (*smiling*): That's a flattering sound!

FIRST CADET: He bores us!

CARBON: But he's still a Gascon.

SECOND CADET: A false one! Do not trust him!

CYRANO (*quickly*): Don't show that you are suffering. Take out your cards, your pipes, your dice! (*They all quickly begin to play their games.*) I will read.

DE GUICHE (*to* CARBON): Ah, good day! (*Looking at the* CADETS) So here are the quarrelsome fellows. Yes, gentlemen, I have heard rumors that you jeer at me. You think a man cannot be a Gascon without being dirt poor? So shall I have you punished by your captain?

CARBON: I am free to do as I wish. And I give no punishments.

DE GUICHE: That will do. (*To the* CADETS) I can ignore your mockery. My way of standing fire is well known. Only yesterday, I drove back the enemy. Like an avalanche I hurled my men down and charged three times.

CYRANO (*without looking up from his book*): Don't forget your white scarf.

DE GUICHE (*pleased*): Oh, so you heard about that, too? I was in danger of being captured or shot. But I had the good sense to take off the scarf that showed my rank. I dropped it on the ground and was able to slip away without being noticed. Then I came back with my men and beat the Spaniards. What do you think of that?

CYRANO: You and I have different ideas of courage, sir. If I had been there when the scarf was dropped, I would have picked it up and put it on.

DE GUICHE: That's Gascon boasting!

CYRANO: Boasting? Lend me the scarf, and on this very night I shall wear it and lead the assault.

DE GUICHE: You know very well my scarf remained by the river in a place under heavy enemy fire. No one can go and bring it back.

CYRANO (*taking the white scarf from his pocket and handing it to him*): Here it is.

(*Silence. The* CADETS *choke back their laughter.*)

DE GUICHE: Thank you. Now with this piece of white cloth, I can make a necessary signal.

(*He climbs to the rampart and waves the scarf many times.*)

A SENTRY (*on the rampart*): A man down there is running away.

DE GUICHE: He's a false Spanish spy. He performs a great service for us. He carries whatever information I give him to the enemy. Then we can influence their decisions. Last night, the marshal took many troops with him to Dourlens, where our supplies are. He is making one mighty effort to get food for us. But it has left the enemy a fine opportunity to attack us.

CARBON: If the Spaniards knew, it would be grave.

DE GUICHE: They do know. They are going to attack. My spy came to warn me. He said they shall attack our weakest post, wherever that is. I told him to watch our lines, and I would signal him from that post. So here I am.

CARBON (*to the* CADETS): Gentlemen, get ready.

DE GUICHE: It will be in an hour. You will fight until the last of you is killed.

CYRANO: Ah, is that your revenge?

DE GUICHE: It is true that if I had liked you, I would not have chosen you and your men.

CYRANO (*bowing*): Allow me to express my gratitude, sir.

(DE GUICHE *goes aside with* CARBON. CYRANO *goes to* CHRISTIAN, *who has remained still, with his arms folded.*)

CHRISTIAN (*shaking his head*): Oh, Roxane. . . I wish I could put my heart's farewell into one last letter.

CYRANO: I suspected the end might come today. (*Takes the letter from his pocket*) So I have written your farewell.

CHRISTIAN (*takes the letter and opens it. Begins to read and stops suddenly.*): What is this—this little stain? It is a tear!

CYRANO (*takes the letter back*): A poet is caught at his own game—that's the charm. The note was so touching, it made me weep to write it.

CHRISTIAN: Weep?

CYRANO: Yes—because to die is not terrible. But never to see her again—that is horrible. I'll never see her—you'll never see. . .

CHRISTIAN (*snatches the letter back*): Give me that note!

(*A distant noise is heard in the camp.*)

A Sentry (*shouts from the rampart*): A carriage.

(*Everyone rushes to look.*)

All: Did you hear what the driver said? He said, "King's service!"

Carbon: Hats off, all of you!

De Guiche: King's service! Clear the way!

(*The carriage enters rapidly. It is covered with mud and dust. The curtains are drawn. It stops short.*)

Carbon: Beat a salute! (*The drums roll.*)

De Guiche: Lower the steps!

(*Two men rush to the coach. The carriage door opens.*)

Roxane (*jumping from the coach*): Good morning!

(*The sound of a woman's voice causes all the bowed heads to look up in amazement.*)

## Scene 2

*The camp of the Gascony Guards.*

De Guiche: Service of the king? You?

Roxane: Of the only king—Love!

Cyrano: Good God!

Christian (*rushing to her*): You! Why?

Roxane: The siege was too long!

Cyrano (*aside*): Shall I look at her?

De Guiche: You can't stay here!

Roxane: Yes, I can! Would you please bring me a drum to sit on? (*It is brought.*) Thank you.

CYRANO: This is madness! Where the devil could you have passed through safely?

ROXANE: Through the Spanish lines! I simply drove along as fast as possible. If a Spanish officer gave me a suspicious look, I put on my sweetest smile at the door. And because, with all due respect to the French, Spanish gentlemen are the most gallant in the world, I was able to pass.

CHRISTIAN: But. . .

DE GUICHE: You must depart!

ROXANE: But why?

CHRISTIAN (*embarrassed*): Because. . .in the next half hour. . .

ROXANE: You are going to fight.

ALL: Oh, no!

ROXANE: This is my husband. Let me be killed with him!

DE GUICHE (*in despair*): This is a very dangerous post.

CYRANO (*to* DE GUICHE): Yes, thanks to you.

ROXANE (*to* DE GUICHE): Ah, then you wish me to become a widow? Now, I am mad. I'm not going away. Besides, I have on a hat which will look good in battle. Now, don't you think it's time for Mr. de Guiche to go away? They might begin!

DE GUICHE: This is all too much. I am going to inspect my cannons. I will return. You still have time to change your mind!

ROXANE: Never!

(DE GUICHE *goes out.*)

CHRISTIAN (*pleading*): Roxane!

ROXANE: No!

FIRST CADET (*to the others*): She will stay.

ALL (*rushing about to make themselves more presentable.*): A comb—A brush—Some soap. My clothes are torn, give me a needle. A razor!

FIRST CADET (*to the others*): I should die without regret, having seen this pretty face. If I only had one small bite to eat.

CARBON (*angrily, having overheard*): Shame—to speak of eating when a fair lady—

ROXANE: But I'm hungry, too. It must be the camp's cool air. Pate, cold chicken, and wine—that is my choice. Would you be kind enough to bring them?

A CADET: Bring them? Where can we get them?

ROXANE (*calmly*): From my carriage.

ALL: What!

ROXANE: But they must be boned and carved and served. Look at my coachman a little closer, gentlemen. You'll recognize a valuable man. Every sauce shall be served hot, if you like.

ALL (*rushing toward the carriage*): It is Ragueneau! (*Loud cheers*)

RAGUENEAU (*standing on the driver's seat*): Gentlemen! The Spaniards failed to see the feast, when the feast of beauty passed. Distracted by beauty, they did not notice the beast! (*Picks up a roast pig on a tray and holds it up*)

(*Applause. The tray is passed around.*)

CYRANO (*softly, to* CHRISTIAN): I beg you, one word!

ROXANE (t*ossing a folded tablecloth to* CYRANO): Make yourself useful—unfold this cloth.

CYRANO (*to* CHRISTIAN, *while they spread the table-cloth*): I must speak to you before you speak to her!

ROXANE (*pouring wine and serving food*): Everything for the Gascons! And if de Guiche comes, he comes uninvited.

CYRANO (*aside*): I adore her!

LE BRET (*returning from giving a loaf of bread to the* SENTRY *on the rampart*): Here comes de Guiche!

CYRANO: Quick, hide the bottles, plates, baskets. Let us show nothing! (*To* RAGUENEAU) Back to your driver's seat. Is everything hidden?

(*Everything disappears.* DE GUICHE *enters briskly—and stops suddenly, sniffing. Silence.*)

DE GUICHE: Something smells good.

FIRST CADET (*casually singing*): Tra-la-la. . .

DE GUICHE (*looking at him*): You're in a fine mood.

FIRST CADET: It is because danger is near.

DE GUICHE (*calling* CARBON, *to give an order*): Here, Captain I. . . (*Looks at him.*) You're cheerful, too!

CARBON: Well, I. . .

DE GUICHE: There is one cannon left. I've had it brought there. (*Points to corner*) Use it if you need it. (*To* ROXANE) Well, what have you decided?

ROXANE: I shall remain.

DE GUICHE: In that case, give me a musket!

CARBON: What?

DE GUICHE: I shall remain, too.

CYRANO: At last, sir, you show pure bravery!

DE GUICHE: I never leave a woman in danger.

SECOND CADET (*to the first*): I think we might give him something to eat.

(*All the food reappears as if by magic.*)

DE GUICHE (*his eyes lighting up*): Food! (*Then controlling himself, with dignity*) Do you think I will eat your left-overs? (*Proudly*) I shall fight, fasting.

FIRST CADET (*delighted*): Spoken like a true Gascon!

DE GUICHE (*laughing*): I?

FIRST CADET: He's one of us.

(*The cadets begin to dance.* DE GUICHE *asks* ROXANE *to go with him to inspect the ramparts. She takes his hand, and they leave.*)

CHRISTIAN (*rushing to* CYRANO): Speak—quick!

CYRANO: If Roxane should speak to you of letters. . .

CHRISTIAN: Go on!

CYRANO: Don't be so stupid as to show surprise.

CHRISTIAN: At what?

CYRANO: You have written her more often than you think.

CHRISTIAN: What?

CYRANO: I took it upon myself—I was the interpreter of your passion. I sometimes wrote without telling you.

CHRISTIAN: But how did you manage it? We are blockaded.

CYRANO: Oh, before dawn I was able to get through.

CHRISTIAN (*folding his arms*): How often have I been writing? Twice a week? Three times? Four?

CYRANO: More than that.

CHRISTIAN (*violently*): And that made you so drunk with sheer delight that you braved death—

CYRANO (*seeing* ROXANE *returning*): Hush! Not in front of her.

(*He quickly returns to his tent.*)

# Scene 3

*The camp of the Gascony Guards.*

ROXANE (*running to* CHRISTIAN): Now, Christian!

CHRISTIAN: So tell me why you traveled such frightful roads, passed the enemy, to join me here.

ROXANE: It's your fault if I have risked these dangers. Your letters made my head spin. Think of how many you've written to me in the last month. Each one more beautiful than the last!

CHRISTIAN: What—for a few little love letters. . .

ROXANE: Yes! I've adored you since that evening when you hid under my window and revealed your soul in a way I've never heard before. Your letters for the past month have been in that same voice. And I felt your love, so powerful, so sincere.

CHRISTIAN: Powerful and sincere?

ROXANE: Oh, yes!

CHRISTIAN: And you have come. . .

ROXANE: I have come to ask your pardon for having insulted you at first. You see, I first loved you only because you were handsome.

CHRISTIAN: And now?

ROXANE: I now love you for your soul alone.

CHRISTIAN (*stepping back*): Oh, Roxane!

ROXANE: I understand. You can't believe such love.

CHRISTIAN: No! It was better before!

ROXANE: I'd love you still, if all your beauty should suddenly vanish.

CHRISTIAN: You mean even if I were ugly?

ROXANE: Yes! I swear it!

CHRISTIAN: God!

ROXANE: What's the matter?

CHRISTIAN (*gently pushing her away*): Nothing. I have to go talk to someone. Wait a moment. (*Goes to* CYRANO'S *tent*) Cyrano!

CYRANO (*coming out of the tent, armed for battle*): What? Why are you pale?

CHRISTIAN: She no longer loves me!

CYRANO: No!

CHRISTIAN: She loves only my soul. That means it's you she loves—and you love her, too.

CYRANO: Yes, it is true!

CHRISTIAN: Tell her so.

CYRANO: No!

CHRISTIAN: Why not?

CYRANO: Look at my face!

CHRISTIAN: She would still love *me* if *I* were ugly.

CYRANO: She told you so?

CHRISTIAN: Yes!

CYRANO: Ah, don't believe such nonsense. Don't take her at her word.

CHRISTIAN: Go and tell her all. Let her decide.

CYRANO: No, not that torture!

CHRISTIAN: Tell her everything!

CYRANO: He insists on tempting me!

CHRISTIAN: I am tired of being my own rival!

CYRANO: He persists. . .

CHRISTIAN: I must be loved for myself, or not at all. I must go to the end of our lines. Speak to her while I'm gone. Let her choose between us.

CYRANO: It will be you!

CHRISTIAN: I hope so! (*Calls*) Roxane!

CYRANO: No! No!

ROXANE: What is it?

CHRISTIAN: Cyrano has something important to tell you—

(*She turns to* CYRANO. CHRISTIAN *exits.*)

# Scene 4

*The camp of the Gascony Guards.*

ROXANE: You have something important to say?

CYRANO: It was nothing. You should know— Christian makes much out of little.

ROXANE (*anxiously*): He did not believe what I said just now. I could see he had his doubts.

CYRANO (*taking her hand*): But did you really tell the truth?

ROXANE: Yes, I should love him even—(*She hesitates a second.*)

CYRANO (*smiling sadly*): It troubles you to say the word in front of me?

ROXANE: But—

CYRANO: You would love him even if he were *ugly*?

ROXANE: Yes! (*Several musket shots are heard.*) Ah, wait! They are firing!

CYRANO: You still would love him?

ROXANE: Yes, and even more!

CYRANO (*aside*): My God, perhaps it is true. Perhaps happiness is for me. (*To* ROXANE) Listen, Roxane. . .

LE BRET (*calls in a low voice*): Cyrano!

CYRANO (*turning around*): What?

LE BRET: Hush! (*Whispers something to him*)

CYRANO (*letting go of* ROXANE's *hand with a cry*): Oh!

ROXANE: What's the matter?

CYRANO (*aside*): It's all over. I can never tell her!

ROXANE: What's happened?

CYRANO (*stopping her as she is about to rush forward*): Nothing!

(*Some* CADETS *enter. They are hiding something they are carrying. They form a group to prevent* ROXANE *from approaching.*)

ROXANE: But what were you going to say to me before?

CYRANO: Nothing! I swear that Christian's spirit and soul were. . . are the greatest. . .

ROXANE: Were? (*Rushes forward and pushes*

CADETS *aside. Sees* CHRISTIAN l*ying wrapped in his cloak.*) Christian!

LE BRET (*to* CYRANO): The enemy's first shot!

(ROXANE *kneels beside* CHRISTIAN. *More shots. Drums.*)

CARBON (*sword in hand*): It is the attack. To arms!

(*Followed by the* CADETS, *he climbs over the rampart.*)

ROXANE: Christian!

CHRISTIAN (*in a dying voice*): Roxane. . .

CYRANO (*speaking softly in* CHRISTIAN'S *ear*): I have told her all. She still loves you.

(CHRISTIAN *closes his eyes.*)

ROXANE: Yes, my love? I feel his cheek cold against mine. What's this? A letter for me! (*Opens it*)

CYRANO (*aside*): My letter!

CARBON: Fire! (*Shots, sounds of battle*)

CYRANO (*trying to draw away*): Roxane, the attack has begun!

ROXANE: Stay a little longer. He was a wonderful being, wasn't he?

CYRANO: Yes, Roxane.

ROXANE: A poet to adore! (*Throwing herself to the ground*) He's dead!

CYRANO (*aside, drawing his sword*): There is nothing left for me to do but to die. For without knowing it, she is mourning for me!

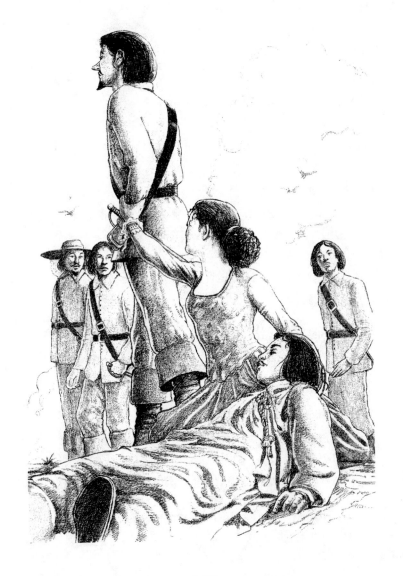

DE GUICHE (*reappearing on the rampart, wounded*): The promised signal! The French will quickly reach the camp with supports. Hold out a little longer.

ROXANE: On his letter, blood and tears. (*Softly kissing the letter*) His blood! His tears! (*She faints.*)

DE GUICHE: Hold your ground!

CYRANO (*to DE GUICHE*): You have proved your courage, sir. (*Points to ROXANE*) Escape with her.

DE GUICHE (*runs to ROXANE and carries her away in his arms*): So be it! But we can still win if you can gain time.

(CYRANO *rushing forward, is stopped by* CARBON, *covered with blood.*)

CARBON: Our line is broken. I've had two wounds.

CYRANO: Don't give up. I have two deaths to avenge—Christian's and my own.

(*Sounds of battle. They exit. The curtain falls.*)

# ACT 5

## Cyrano's Gazette

*This act takes place 15 years later in the garden of a church convent in Paris. Roxane went to live there after Christian's death. Cyrano comes to visit her every week to bring her the latest news from the city. He is poor and often hungry, although Roxane is not aware of this.*

*Cyrano arrives for his weekly visit. He and Roxane have a long talk in which the secrets of the past finally come out in the open.*

# Scene 1

*The garden of the convent. As the curtain rises,* Nuns *are coming and going.* Sister Marthe *and* Sister Claire *are seated on a bench with* Mother Marguérite. *Between the bench and a tree stands a large embroidery table.*

Sister Marthe (*to* Mother Marguérite): Sister Claire has stopped in front of the mirror twice to look at her headdress.

Mother Marguérite (*to* Sister Claire): That was naughty.

Sister Claire: But I saw Sister Marthe take a plum from the tart this morning.

Mother Marguérite: Another naughty deed! (*Sternly*) I'll tell Mr. Cyrano this evening.

Sister Claire: No! He'll make fun of us. He'll call us silly and greedy.

Mother Marguérite (*smiling.*): And rightly so.

SISTER CLAIRE: Hasn't he been here every Saturday for the past ten years, Mother Marguérite?

MOTHER MARGUÉRITE: Longer than that! Ever since his cousin Roxane came to us 15 years ago, mixing her black mourning veil with our linen caps.

ALL THE NUNS: He is so delightful—so amusing. Such a nice man. We all like him.

SISTER MARTHE: But he's not a very good Catholic!

MOTHER MARGUÉRITE: Never fear. God must know him well.

SISTER MARTHE: Every Saturday when he comes, he says to me, "Sister, I ate meat yesterday!"

MOTHER MARGUÉRITE: Does he tell you that? Well, the last time he had eaten nothing for two days.

SISTER MARTHE: Oh!

MOTHER MARGUÉRITE: He's rather poor.

SISTER MARTHE: Who told you so?

MOTHER MARGUÉRITE: Mr. Le Bret.

SISTER MARTHE: Doesn't anyone assist him?

MOTHER MARGUÉRITE: No, he would be offended.

(ROXANE *appears in the background. She is dressed in black, with a widow's cap and long veils.* DE GUICHE, *looking old but elegant, walks beside her.*)

MOTHER MARGUÉRITE: Let us go inside. Madame Roxane is walking in the garden with a visitor.

SISTER MARTHE (*to* SISTER CLAIRE): It's the Marshal Duke de Grammont, isn't it?

SISTER CLAIRE (*looking*): Yes, I think so.

SISTER MARTHE: He hasn't come to see her for months.

OTHER NUNS: He has been very much occupied. The court—the army. . .

(*The* NUNS *exit.*)

# Scene 2

*The park of the convent.* ROXANE *and* THE DUKE DE GRAMMONT (*formerly* DE GUICHE) *stand near the embroidery table.*

THE DUKE: And so you will stay here forever, in mourning?

ROXANE: Forever.

THE DUKE (*after a moment of silence*): Have you forgiven me?

ROXANE: Yes, since I've been here I have.

(*Another silence*)

THE DUKE: You love him even in death?

ROXANE: Sometimes, it seems to me that he is only half dead. It's as if our hearts are together and his love floats around me, very much alive!

THE DUKE: Does Cyrano come to see you?

ROXANE: Yes, he visits regularly and tells me

about the events of the week. He's become my newspaper. . . my gazette. (LE BRET *appears on the steps.*) Ah, here's Le Bret. How is our friend, Cyrano?

LE BRET: He is ill.

THE DUKE: Oh!

ROXANE: He exaggerates!

LE BRET: Cyrano is living alone and in poverty. His writings constantly make new enemies for him.

ROXANE: But his sword inspires the deepest fear. No one will ever get the better of him.

THE DUKE (*shaking his head*): Who knows?

LE BRET: What I fear is not the attacks. Loneliness, hunger, the cold of December creeping into his dark room. These are the assassins that will kill him.

THE DUKE: Don't feel too sorry for him. He has lived without compromise. He is free in both thoughts and action. (*Bowing to* ROXANE) I must go. Good-bye.

ROXANE: I'll walk you out.

THE DUKE (*stops as he is about to leave*): Mr. Le Bret, may I have a word with you? (*To* LE BRET, softly) Your friend is hated by many people. Tell him not to go out very often and to be very careful.

ROXANE (*to a* NUN *coming toward her*): Yes?

SISTER MARTHE: Ragueneau would like to see you.

**81**

ROXANE: Bring him in. (*To* THE DUKE *and* LE BRET) He's come to complain about his poverty.

RAGUENEAU (*entering quickly*): Ah, Madame. (*Sees* LE BRET) Sir!

ROXANE (*smiling*): Tell your misfortunes to Le Bret. I'll be back soon.

RAGUENEAU: But Madame. . .

(ROXANE *leaves with* THE DUKE. RAGUENEAU *goes to* LE BRET.)

RAGUENEAU: Since you are here, I would rather not have her know about it. I was going to visit Cyrano just now. I saw him come out of his house. As he turned the corner of the street, a lackey dropped a piece of firewood on him from a window.

LE BRET: The cowards—poor Cyrano!

RAGUENEAU: Our friend, sir, our poet. He was lying on the ground with a big gash in his head.

LE BRET: Is he dead?

RAGUENEAU: No, but Heavens!

LE BRET: Did you call a doctor?

RAGUENEAU: One came out of kindness.

LE BRET: What did the doctor say?

RAGUENEAU: I don't remember very clearly. He said something about fever—the brain. Let us go to him at once! There is no one at his side. He may die, sir!

LE BRET: Come! It is shorter past the chapel.

(ROXANE *appears on the steps. She sees* LE BRET *rushing out.*)

ROXANE: Mr. LE BRET!

(LE BRET *and* RAGUENEAU *exit without answering.*)

# Scene 3

*The garden of the convent.*

ROXANE: How beautiful this last day of September is. (*She sits down in front of her embroidery table.* SISTER CLAIRE *comes out of the house and brings a large armchair under the tree.*)

ROXANE: Thank you, Sister.

SISTER CLAIRE: Mr. Bergerac has arrived.

ROXANE (*without turning around*): Late for the first time in 15 years! (*She continues her work.* CYRANO *is very pale, and his hat is pulled down over his eyes.*)

CYRANO: Yes, I am annoyed. I was delayed by—

ROXANE: By what?

CYRANO: By an untimely visitor.

ROXANE: Tell me the latest news. Where is my gazette?

CYRANO (*growing more pale, struggling against the pain*): At the Queen's ball on Sunday, they burned 763 white wax candles; they say our troops have beaten John of Austria

in battle; four witches have been hanged. On Monday—nothing.

(*He closes his eyes. His head drops forward. Silence.* ROXANE t*urns and looks at him. She stands up in alarm.*)

ROXANE: Has he fainted? (*Runs to him*) Cyrano!

CYRANO (*opening his eyes, distantly*): No! It's nothing. Go back to your chair.

ROXANE: But you. . .

CYRANO: It is only the wound I received at Arras. Sometimes it. . . you know. . .

ROXANE: My poor friend! Each of us has a wound. I have mine, still unhealed. (*Puts her hand to her heart*) It is here under this letter with its yellowed paper stained with tears and blood.

CYRANO: His letter! Did you not tell me that someday I might read it?

ROXANE: Would you like to read it now?

CYRANO: Yes, I would.

(ROXANE *hands him the letter. She returns to her embroidery table and begins to put it away.*)

CYRANO (*reading*): "Farewell, Roxane, I am going to die!—"

ROXANE (*stopping in surprise*): Reading aloud?

CYRANO (*continuing*): "My soul is still heavy with unspoken love, and I am dying. Never again shall my eyes delight . . ."

ROXANE: How well you read his letter!

CYRANO: . . . in each of your graceful movements. I want to cry out. . ."

ROXANE (*troubled*): How well you read it!

(*The twilight is turning to darkness.*)

CYRANO: ". . . Good-bye!"

ROXANE: You read it—in a voice that I have heard before.

(*She approaches him without his noticing her. She stands behind his chair and looks at the letter. The darkness increases. She puts her hand on his shoulder.*)

ROXANE: You can't read now? It is dark. You recite this from memory. (*He turns around in alarm, then bows his head.*) And for 15 years, you've played the part of an old friend who came to amuse me!

CYRANO: Roxane!

ROXANE: It was you!

CYRANO: No, Roxane, no!

ROXANE: I ought to have guessed when you spoke my name.

CYRANO: I swear to you. . .

ROXANE: I see through this fraud. The letters were yours. . .

CYRANO: No! I did not love you!

ROXANE: You loved me.

CYRANO (*in a weakening voice*): No!

Roxane: Already you say it more softly. Ah, how many things are dead, how many things are born! Why have you kept silent for 15 years, knowing that the letters and the tears were yours?

Cyrano (*folds the letter*): The blood was his.

# Scene 4

*The garden of the convent.* Le Bret *and* Ragueneau *enter, running.*

Le Bret: What madness! I was sure of it—there he is. (*To* Roxane) He's killing himself by leaving his bed.

Cyrano: Roxane, I have not finished giving you the weekly news. "Today, Saturday the 26th, an hour before dinner, Mr. de Bergerac was found murdered."

(*He takes off his hat showing the bandages on his head.*)

Roxane: Cyrano! What have they done to you? Why?

Cyrano: "Slain by a hero, with the sword point in my heart!" Yes. Fate is a great jester. Here I am, killed from behind, hit with a block of wood. I have failed in everything—even in death.

(*The chapel bell rings. The* Nuns *are seen in the background, going to mass.*)

Roxane (*rising to call for help*): Sister, Sister!

Cyrano (*holding her back*): Don't go for anyone. When you return, I shall have gone away.

ROXANE: I love you! Live!

CYRANO: No! In the fairy tale, when she says, "I love you," the prince's ugliness melts like snow in the sunshine. As you see, I remain the same.

ROXANE: I have been the cause of your unhappiness!

CYRANO: On the contrary. Thanks to you I have had a woman's friendship to soften my loneliness.

ROXANE: I loved but one single being—and I must lose him twice!

CYRANO: Please do not grieve less for the handsome and noble Christian. All I ask is that when my body lies cold in death, you'll give a double meaning to those black veils. And you'll mourn for me a little when you mourn for him.

ROXANE: I swear it!

(CYRANO *is shaken and rises quickly.*)

CYRANO: No, not there! Not in a chair! (*They move towards him.*) Do not support me! (*He leans against a tree.*) Nothing but the tree! (*Silence*) He is coming. I will await him standing—sword in hand! (*Draws his sword*)

LE BRET: Cyrano!

ROXANE (*half fainting*): Cyrano!

(*All draw back in terror.*)

CYRANO: I believe that he dares to look at my nose. (*Lifts his sword*) What's that you say? It's useless? I know it! But one does not fight with hope of success. It is a much finer thing when it is useless. What are those? Ah, I recognize you—my old enemies! (*He strikes the air with his sword.*) Compromise! Prejudice! Cowardice! (*Thrusts again*) Shall I make peace with you? Never! I know in the end, you may win. Yet I fight, I fight! Yes, you have taken everything from me—the laurel and the rose. But in spite of you, there is one thing I take with me tonight. It is free from creases or stains. (*Springs forward with his sword raised*) That is—

(*His sword drops from his hand. He stumbles and falls into the arms of* LE BRET *and* RAGUENEAU.)

ROXANE (*bending down and kissing him on the forehead*): What is it?

CYRANO (*opening his eyes and smiling*): My unsoiled pen.

(*The curtain falls.*)